WLM228
DAV

PRAISE FOR MARTIN DAVIES' PREVIOUS BOOK

"SOD IT! *The Depression 'Virus' and how to deal with it*"

"A comprehensive resource for people who are affected by depression"
(Practice Nursing magazine)

"Having worked with depression in primary care for over 10 years, it has been a constant frustration to me that no-one has combined the wisdom of the experience of depression with the humour and self-deprecation needed for recovery. This skinny little tome changes all that. Humour is anti-viral... buy this book for sustained immunity!!" **(P. Rice, UK)**

"This is really helpful for anyone who suffers from depression themselves, or has family members, friends or colleagues who suffer. It is easy to read and 'dip into' (really important as the ability to concentrate tends to go while depressed) while being very informative and based on research. The diary templates are really helpful, especially 7. The cartoons are really fabulous and convey so much information so simply" **(P. Connell, UK)**

"If this book had been around during my years of coping with depression I would have been able to explain to the people nearest to me exactly what I was going through and not felt that I was some kind of freak, drop out, a changed person. I am convinced that the illustrations would have brought a smile to my face and the whole world (well, my world) wouldn't have been so bad" **(S. Barker, UK)**

"This is a very accessible read that is brought to life by the perceptive and humourous cartoons. Conceptualising depression as a "virus" is an interesting and visual way to convey the debilitating experience. It clarifies fact from fiction and lets you dip into features that may be pertinent to you in surviving depression" **(M. Daniel, UK)**

SOD IT! Books

Is the book imprint of Talking Life, specialists in Health information CDs and audio cassettes and designers of training for healthcare and other public sector staff. Self-help titles include: Depression, Anxiety, Pain Management, Sleep Problems, Bereavement, Stress, Headaches & Migraine, Tranquilliser Addiction, Self-Esteem and Assertiveness Skills. There is also a popular range of relaxation programmes. For latest information of the Sod It! Books range of books and our Talking Life range of CDs and Cassettes, telephone us on **0151 632 0662**, write to us at **PO Box 1, Wirral CH47 7DD** or visit our websites:
www.sod-itbooks.co.uk and **www.talkinglife.co.uk**

SOD IT ALL!

How to Deal with the Stress 'Virus' in your Life
by Martin Davies

(Thanks to Wendy Bennett for editing this book.
Her sense of humour is now seriously frayed)

Published by Sod It! Books
PO Box 1
Wirral CH47 7DD, England

ISBN 9781901910087

Printed and bound in Great Britain by
Bookmarque, Croydon, Surrey

FOR MORE INFORMATION ABOUT SOD IT! BOOKS
(+44) 0151-632-0662
www.sod-itbooks.co.uk
www.talkinglife.co.uk

SOD IT ALL!

How to deal with the Stress 'Virus' in your life

MARTIN DAVIES, RMN., Dip. C.P.N.

ABOUT THE AUTHOR

From a psychiatric nursing background, Martin has worked in the field of mental health since the mid-seventies. Son of an alcoholic mother and having lost both his parents at an early age, Martin experienced infection from the stress virus at perhaps too early an age. Professionally he realised that the stress virus was responsible for a range of mental illnesses, and triggered many others. Also, witnessing the effect on colleagues and going through many of the dreaded NHS reforms, the stress virus was a constant threat.

Going through a traumatic divorce and experiencing the effects that 'toxic' partners have on one's own emotional health (and on children), Martin developed, through his own experiences of 'Burnout', a range of training courses aimed at helping others. This book is the result of many years work, and Martin only illustrates and suggests the things that he himself uses, or has used to cope and manage stress. This book is also an adjunct to his previous book "SOD IT!" which examines the other dreaded **depression virus**. A freelance illustrator, he communicates his messages through humour and empathy - your sense of humour (or what's left of it) is essential, for both understanding the book as well as for coping.

INTRODUCTION

STRESS! A single word with a range of functions, some good, some bad. Without stress we would still be in the prehistoric swamp! Animals experience stress, without it they would be sitting targets for their prey or would die from hunger. For humans, 'Stress' is a word that has become almost fashionable, yet is still misinterpreted and grossly misunderstood. It is a strong, instinctual mechanism and it can have a major influence on the individual and on others. The family of stress 'viruses' spreads quickly and can be harboured in the body for a long time. A motivator and inspirational friend, it is also capable of destroying lives, blighting families and robbing many people of a future. There is no 'vaccine'! 'Inoculation' and the 'cure' must come from within. Some people manage it well, whilst others have to learn to live with it and manage its effects on a moment to moment basis. Understanding stress is a key to coping with it. **This book can help you to do that.**

THE TRICKY TRIO

STRESS IS:

The normal response to stimulus which is desirable and indeed motivating. The alarm clock in the morning gives our first 'wake-up' call to our adrenal glands - kicking them into action for the events of the day. Without this we would be inanimate objects! We **NEED** a certain amount of it. It's when **stress** turns into **DIS**stress that things start to get uncomfortable and if we push this too far, for too long, we can move towards the more serious state of **ANXIETY**. Stressful events have psychological, behavioural and physical effects and symptoms, which usually only last a few moments, a few minutes, hours, days or a week or so.

ANXIETY IS:

Not to be mixed up with 'anxious'. We **ALL** get anxious once in a while. Nothing wrong or bad about that! But **prolonged, sustained** and **increasing** anxiousness can lead to an anxiety illness. The state of anxiety is an **ILLNESS** that needs treatment. Anxiety states are overwhelming feelings and an inability to cope. Prolonged anxiety and stress can lead to another disabling state: **DEPRESSION**.

DEPRESSION IS:

Anything from a normal lowering of mood, from which we can all suffer, to extreme mood swings and dysfunction (an inability to carry out day to day activities, that were once easy). This can be caused by an accumulation of difficult life events or prolonged distress - wearing a person down to the point of physical and emotional exhaustion. Anyone can become depressed. Depression is not just feeling 'blue', it is an overpowering bleakness that has well-defined symptoms.

THE STRESS VIRUS

(Latin: STIMULATIS MAXIMUS)

"What's the problem with STRESS?"

Nothing, actually. Stress is perfectly normal and every human being has it - without it we'd be unmoving objects in a cabbage field! In fact, if anyone ever tells you that they "never suffer from stress", then they are clinically dead! It's normal, we need it, it motivates us and inspires us to do greater things. So, in fact, the **STRESS VIRUS**, in small doses HELPS us. It only becomes a problem when it multiplies into great numbers for a length of time.

It's when stress BREEDS, into large numbers, for too long that you need to beware!

Too much of the virus for long periods creates **OVERLOAD**. Overload is when stress turns into **DIS**-stress - an uncomfortable (and generally unproductive) state that, if left unchecked, can lead to all sorts of psychological and physical problems. In the short-term there are few effects that cause any problems - but allow this little blighter to increase in numbers….and you might wish you'd have kept it in check! The stress virus **LOVES** people who are:

o Run down (physically and emotionally)
o Over-worked (and take little rest)
o Experiencing problems (and not addressing them)
o Isolated, lonely, miserable (who don't share problems)
o Experiencing long-term illnesses (and painful conditions)
o Tense and uptight individuals (prone to over-reactions)

Small doses of stress = stimulation!

Stress chemicals are naturally occurring chemical stimulants (natural stress juices!) which essentially motivate us. They:

o   Get us up in the morning
o   Help us to DO things in the day
o   Generate ideas and creativity
o   Help us to be productive in life and in work
o   Produce excitement and motivate us

These chemicals have effects on other (natural) chemicals in the body and mind, such as endorphins (often experienced as a 'high' after activity or exercise), and serotonin (a mood chemical giving us a sense of pleasure, contentment and an overall sense of well-being and happiness).

Effects of TOO MUCH stress juices on the BODY
(If sustained over time)

o   Immune system breakdown
o   Raised blood pressure
o   Fatigue, tiredness, lack of energy
o   Increased headaches and other minor ailments
o   Increased muscle tension leading to aches and pains
o   Changes in sleep and appetite

Effects of TOO MUCH stress juices on the MIND
(If sustained over time)

o   Poor concentration (short-term memory loss)
o   Irritability and mood swings
o   Pre-occupying thoughts (ruminations)
o   Inability to keep things clear and in perspective
o   Withdrawal and/or angry outbursts
o   Anxiety and depression
o   Poor sleep and restlessness

"SOMATISATION"

One of the most common signs of stress-related problems, anxiety and depression. This is when you build up tension/unpleasant feeling (anger/stress/resentment/rage/etc) or store unresolved issues up in your mind, over a period of time, and thereby significantly change the <u>body's chemistry</u> to a point where **physical symptoms** start to appear (headaches/muscle pain/palpitations/chest pain etc).

Men do this much more than women. Perhaps this is because men are less likely to share their built up worries and concerns. This bottling up has a nasty habit of eventually turning into an unstable and erupting **VOLCANO!** Somatisation is not experiencing **imaginary** pain, it is indeed <u>real</u> pain and discomfort, it's just that the cause is not illness or disease - but built-up emotional pain.

<u>PAINFUL people are often....PAIN-FULL!</u>

The *ERUPTING VOLCANO* Syndrome:

By bottling things up or not being able to resolve issues, a **pressure** has built up inside that is difficult to contain.

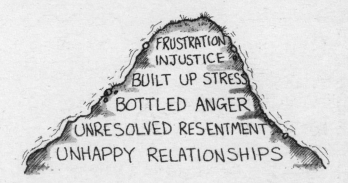

Just like shaking a fizzy drink and keeping the lid on, huge pressure, when released, <u>**explodes**</u> onto those around.

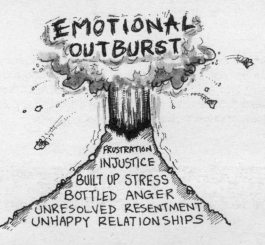

The STRESS CURVE

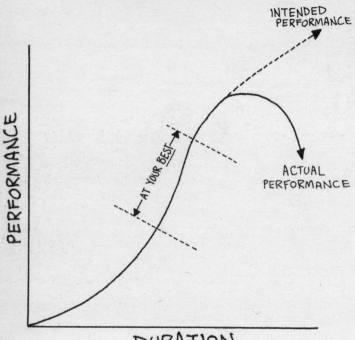

Researchers have long understood that there is a pattern to stress in all of us. The above diagram illustrates how a small amount of stress helps us - but if increased and sustained causes a major drop in performance and ultimately to possible 'Stress **BURNOUT**'. We all move up and down this curve every day - consider where YOU are? Pushing yourself too far up the curve, without proper breaks, can lead to chronic under-performance, illness and a sense of failure. Keeping within your limits improves functioning.

The STRESS POOL

Looking at it another (more visual) way - imagine a **swimming pool**; a little paddle in the shallow end is invigorating, pleasant and enjoyable (even for non-swimmers). However, as we get deeper, it becomes more overwhelming, <u>harder to swim</u>. Even great swimmers need a rest! There comes a point - even for the best of us, when we need to get out for a 'breather'. Some people need to get out completely. Without such rests we can become over-stretched - burnt out - and <u>**drown**</u>!

<u>This is why we need regular breaks!</u>

Common signs of STRESS

Anyone can experience any of these at any time, causing neither harm nor major discomfort. They may last for a few moments, a few minutes or for a few hours:

Physical

headaches
palpitations
hot sweats
faint feelings
weakness
tired / fatigue
dry mouth
apprehension
trembling
numbness
tingling sensations
sleep disturbance
appetite change
muscle tension
muscular aches/pains
restlessness / fidgeting
breathlessness / tight chest

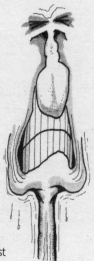

Psychological

irritability / mood swings
poor concentration
poor co-ordination / clumsiness
preoccupying thoughts
impulsiveness / over reaction
worry / over-concern
loss of control
loss of confidence
anticipation of failure
worrying about the future
guilt / worrying over past
poor short-term memory
anger outbursts
emotional withdrawal
lowered self-esteem
pre-occupation with health
tearfulness
loss of patience and tolerance

It's when you experience these sorts of signs for days, weeks, months or constantly, that you really need to make changes or seek help. Maintaining such symptoms can cause major health problems such as heart disease, and can trigger irritable bowel syndrome and other problems. Psychologically these **will** wear you down!

In the short-term though, these cause NO HARM!

The importance of
UNDERSTANDING!

If you don't fully understand your symptoms, it's easy to see why some people <u>mis-interpret what's going on inside their body</u>. It is all too easy to link one or two symptoms together, and come up with something that is simply not true.

> ...tingling fingers.... short of breath...palpitations... sweating...chest pain...

> I'm having a HEART ATTACK!!!

Knowing the **FACTS** is the difference between being <u>scared out of your wits</u> and coping. These symptoms are all perfectly normal bodily signs - the human body is built to react in certain ways. You've probably heard of the famous **"Fight or Flight"** process; this is what it is: a series of (normal) body responses to prepare you for either:

<u>**FIGHT:**</u> **Tensing muscles up to confront/altering blood flow/redirecting hormones**

or

<u>**FLIGHT:**</u> **Tensing muscles up to flee/altering blood flow/redirecting hormones**

FIGHT or FLIGHT is NORMAL!

In fact it's desirable! As long as it's for a short period only. But imagine if you got the same 'FIGHT' response, and there was **no** fight; your body would alert itself, with nothing to use up all the chemicals and re-directed blood flow. You would be left with all these **ALERTING** sensations and nothing to do.

This is why, when we do feel tense or over-alert, physical exercise is useful because <u>it gets **RID** of it!</u> If you held onto it for hours and hours you'd become unwell with exhaustion and muscle pain! For those of us (myself included) who don't like exercise, do **ANYTHING** to get rid of it. Go for a walk, listen to some loud music, run up and down the stairs, distract yourself, <u>**don't just frazzle!**</u>

<u>JUST GET RID OF IT; DON'T STORE IT UP!!!!!</u>

Stress can be Helpful

o   Helps us get out of difficult situations quickly
o   React faster when we need to
o   Activates our body to deal with something
o   Gives us physical strength when we really need it
o   Helps us to think quickly
o   Provides us with a strength of emotion to deal with danger

Stress can be Unhelpful

o   It can be inappropriate (occuring at the wrong time!)
o   It can blow things completely out of proportion
o   Causes an over-reaction and therefore causes others pain
o   Stops us sleeping/eating/concentrating properly
o   Makes us alert, keeps us alert, when we don't want it
o   If prolonged, can cause illness and depression

Short-term effects

There are few effects worth worrying about. Your body is built to deal with the short-term effects of stress. OK, so there may be some uncomfortable symptoms (hot, sweaty, light-headed, headache, breathless etc), but these **CAN'T** harm you.

It's important to remember this; if you think these CAN harm you, you'll worry more and provoke **MORE** of a stress response! It's this **mis-belief** that these symptoms can harm you that provokes panic feelings; if you believe this, you'll feel worse! **THESE** are the **FACTS**:

SHORT-TERM STRESS CAUSES NO HARM!

Longer-term effects

This is what you really need to prevent, as the longer-term effects of chronic (on-going) stress can cause problems.

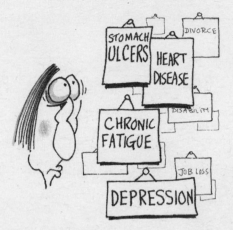

Sustained release of hormones like adrenaline, over time, can lead to secondary effects:

o   Reduce blood circulation (especially to hands/feet)
o   Chronic high blood pressure can cause major circulatory diseases
o   Risk of ulcers and gastric problems
o   Worsening respiratory illnesses (e.g. asthma)
o   Chronic anxiety illness
o   Depression

And of course, the long-term effects on life are just as devastating:

o   Loss of work / employment
o   Relationship breakdown
o   Effects on children and future generations can be awful
o   Chronic worry and inability to cope
o   Depression and suicide

If there's TOO MUCH STRESS JUICE, <u>what do I need?</u>

It's important to try and recognise as <u>**early as possible**</u> if you are <u>**too**</u> stressed (it's uncomfortable and unproductive). There are certain things that you need to do:

o   STOP as soon as possible - stop activity, rest. Or:
o   If you're brimming with excessive energy - get rid of it!
o   Try and relax; from your head down to your toes, slowly relax.
o   Distract your mind onto something (anything) else.
o   Take yourself away; if necessary, go for a short walk.
o   Take one or two slow deep breaths (re-balance your breathing)
o   Go and drink some water (a nice large glass of it), slowly!
o   Go and talk with someone (about this, or anything).
o   Play some music if possible (have you got a personal stereo / mp3?)
o   Write your feelings down, or write about anything. A shopping list?
o   Go and pamper yourself as soon as possible - do something NICE!
o   Go and splash your face with water (it's amazing how distracting this can be)

The point? <u>**Use it up, get rid of it, rebalance**</u> your body and mind. Practise this!

Some people _ARE_ more anxious than others

We are all different, with different personalities and genetic characteristics, living in different circumstances with different pressures. People who have more anxious personalities will naturally feel more anxious than others. Just as some people are optimists and some are pessimists; pessimists are more likely to feel 'down' and more likely to become depressed. Some people are highly efficient whilst some are shambolic and incredibly untidy.

Perhaps it's important, therefore, to appreciate these differences, and not to condemn or belittle others because they are different. Coping with stress is different for us all; some people are lucky not to encounter things that provoke them, whilst others are surrounded by them! Recognise your strengths and weaknesses as well as your limitations. For the rest of us, don't impose on others standards and expectations that are impossible.

Letting the virus get a hold
(and not taking heed or understanding it)

Not 'listening' to your body or mind, and what it is telling you is a sure step to serious infection! Not understanding the FACTS will lead to over-worry and concern, causing MORE infection! The worse you feel and the less you understand, the more you will suffer from stress problems. Learn more about yourself.

Get information - listen to your body!

The "ROAD TO HELL"

Life events and circumstances have a habit of pushing all of us too far at times, a journey that can be all too unpleasant. It's possible to burn out if over-infected by the stress virus. There are phases that, if not recognised, can lead to major physical and psychological problems. If you've walked this road (and fallen off the edge), remember that you are now wiser. You are probably stronger because you've been there. People who have not fallen don't know their limitations. You do.

The perfect breeding ground...
High demands - Unrealistic Expectations

Perhaps this explains, in part, the problems many young people exhibit, leading them to be described as the **"iPod generation"**.

Insecure	Pressurised	Over-taxed	Debt-ridden

Living to such high (unrealistic) expectations is bound to lead to frustration, resentment, disappointment and a sense of failure.

Finding the BALANCE can be difficult

No-one ever really finds the perfect balance, but trying to find a <u>better</u> balance <u>is</u> possible. No-one can do this for you, but they can certainly help. Having a supportive family, partner, employer is great, but not everyone has these. It can be difficult, and it may seem impossible if you have unsupportive and non- understanding people around you.

<u>Some people have to go it alone.</u>

ATTITUDES to stress

Although the word "stress" is more acceptable to use nowadays, there is st[ill] considerable ignorance about its meaning. There is still a lot of negative stigm[a] about it, particularly from some employers. There is a view that it is a "weakness" and that 'strong' people don't suffer from it - **what century are they living in??** Prehistoric attitudes create prehistoric reactions to stress, anxiety and depressio[n]. Poor attitude is down to poor knowledge and lack of respect.

Too <u>much</u> stress for <u>too long</u>

Most people understand that too much stress, for long periods, is inevitably going to cause problems (not that many people actually take heed of this!). Too much pressure, too much stress, increasing distress, lead to overload and, eventually, to illness. Increased changes in the body's chemistry and brain chemistry, physical and mental tiredness all lead to a gradual breakdown in the defences of the body and mind, which in turn produce symptoms. It's **EXHAUSTING!**

<u>HEAVY BAGGAGE HOLDS US BACK, WEIGHS US DOWN!</u>

Too <u>little</u> stress for <u>too long</u>

Just as destructive and distressing is UNDER-load - having too **LITTLE** stimulation. Doing something repetitive and boring, over and over, for long periods can be just as problematic for some people. The body and mind **NEED** arousing, **NEED** pressure, **NEED** to be taxed and tested once in a while. Without these your body slowly chokes up and your mind becomes a vegetable! Just as a car needs regular outings to keep in good condition, so humans **NEED** prodding and moving!

<u>THE BRAIN NEEDS TO BE USED!</u>

Expectations!!!

Not only do others often have unrealistically high expectations of you: - **PARENTS, PARTNER, CHILDREN, EMPLOYER, SOCIETY.** But you might find you often impose unrealistic standards on yourself :

"I must succeed in everything / I must earn as much as I can / I must have everything new / I must look great all the time / I must appear strong"

This 'philosophy' is doomed! It will only create a life that is SO pressured that the only outcome is exhaustion, superficial relationships, huge amounts of time spent on 'impressing' others, and **YOU** will **DISAPPEAR!**

"MUSTERBATION"

Too many **"MUST DOs"** can cause excessive pressure and create unrealistic demands that can only lead to an increasing sense of Failure. Excessive **MUST DO**ing (Musterbation) can be self-imposed.

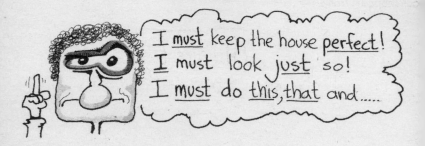

Demanding, unrealistic (and often unreasonable) standards of others, if imposed, will Inevitably lead to friction, conflict and alienation, causing demoralisation.

MUSTERBATION = demanding/controlling/obsessive behaviour based upon unrealistic/unnecessary/unreasonable expectations = excessive pressure.

The emotional
'SHOPPING TROLLEY'

Throughout each day you accumulate a bundle of unsaid things, unresolved issues, resentments or frustrations that are not voiced. You gather these and save them in your shopping trolley.

Where do you take the contents of the shopping trolley and what do you **DO** with them? Often you carry them forward into the next day or next week; the more you pile in the heavier the trolley gets, the harder it is to contain. Keeping these unsaid or unexpressed things inside becomes increasingly difficult, and will have an effect on your emotional and physical health. The trolley can get **OVER-FULL** and will spill out elsewhere! How full is your trolley?

Emptying the trolley!

There comes a point when the contents start to spill out.

Saved 'rubbish' from <u>work</u> gets emptied at <u>home</u>:

Saved 'rubbish' from <u>home</u> gets emptied at <u>work</u>:

We all do this to some extent, but if its not addressed it can cause relationship breakdown, resentment and conflict.

<u>ENSURE YOU HAVE EFFECTIVE DAILY TROLLEY-EMPTYING!</u>

Are there <u>GAINS</u> to you being over-stressed?

Although it might seem odd, for some there are indeed advantages to being 'stressed out' or unwell. For some it might mean that they can get away with not doing some things.

So, consider, is there anything you manage to gain? For example:

o   You get out of participating in certain tasks?
o   You get sympathy from others or get looked after?
o   You can avoid certain people or situations?
o   Others stay away from you (because of your mood); a blessing!
o   You can justify putting off certain things?
o   Others may see you as 'hard working' or 'important' or 'busy'?

The 'Family' of viruses

'Stress' isn't a single entity, it's a family of related viruses, some more helpful than others! Minor infections of the lesser virus is normal and, in fact, desirable! But increasing infection by the less-friendly viruses can lead to pretty dire consequences.

(A minor virus)

(A major virus)

It is a bit like, gobbling up some every-day common bacteria (which we all do every day). This is OK, in fact it all helps to improve overall immunity - it strengthens us! But gobbling up some of the 'nastier' ones can cause illness.

The AROUSAL virus

(Latin: Coma Extracticus)

This is an essential infection. Without It we wouldn't get up in the morning! This little fellow stimulates our ol' adrenal glands just enough to waken us from our comatose sleep. For some, it stimulates a bit too much in the morning - many an argument has been caused by this little bugger! But, for most of us, it's what gets us started in the day, so a little bit of 'stress' is desirable. (Note: people with depression often lose this infection in the morning; it's hard (or impossible) to get up when depressed.)

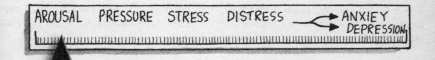

The PRESSURE virus

(Latin: Stimulatus Invigoratus)

Once up from our beds, we need a bit of additional 'oomph!' to get us into a functional state. Without this, any demand other than "Do you want some tea?" would be over-powering and demolishing! Trouble is, we <u>ideally</u> could do with a bit of a **time-lapse** between the arousal phase and the pressure phase, to allow us time to adjust to the activities of the day. But sometimes arousal (wakening up) is followed immediately by pressure: "Mummy - where are my socks??!!" or "Come on - get up **<u>NOW!!</u>**" Try and allow yourself to ease into the day.

<u>**Not everyone bounces out of bed ready for action straight away!**</u>

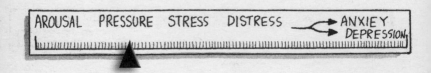

The STRESS virus

(Latin: Stimulatus Maximus)

You are now COOKING! Firing on all cylinders, focussed and dealing with the issues at hand. It might be a bit of a struggle at times but your head is above the water and, most importantly, your <u>sense of humour is still intact!</u> This is a highly productive infection, but the human body (and mind) were **NOT** built to sustain this type of infection for long. It will knock the body and mind out, unless you stop and have breaks. Short-term infection is a **'buzz'**, longer term (and particularly sustained) infections are potential **KILLERS!**

The DISTRESS virus

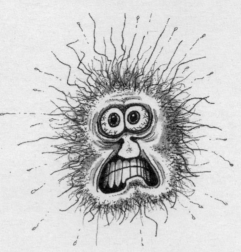

(Latin: Tolerance Absenticus)

Infections with this virus are **not** pleasant, the **buzz** has <u>gone</u>, and so has your sense of humour! This virus starts to impact on work, relationships, family and friends, and erodes your confidence and self-esteem. Dealing with this little sod is a major **BATTLE!** Being in battle for too long is at best wearing and at worst can be traumatising. You may have heard of soldiers, who, if kept in a long state of battle readiness (or battle situation for too long), become **BATTLE-WEARY.** Talk to someone who is in a constant state of distress, or to a depressed person and they are **BATTLE WEARY,** not just battling with job/money/family, but with themselves; they are battling with emotions/guilt/anger/self-doubt/bad thoughts. They are also probably battling with themselves!

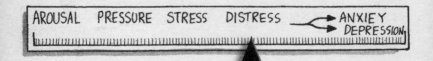

The ANXIETY virus

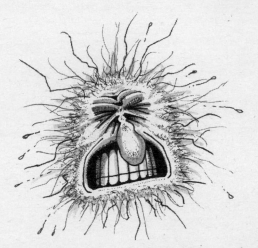

(Latin: Psychologicus Exageratus Maximus)

Not everyone who BURNS OUT or suffers chronlc stress will become infected with THIS nasty virus (<u>and very nasty it is too</u>). Those who do quickly become ill mentally, emotionally and often physically. This is an **illness**, which comes in different forms, **that needs treatment**. <u>Do not EVER underestimate ANXIETY</u>, it interferes with people's lives, including work, relationships, health, children, social life and day to day living. Anxiety causes untold misery and is a major cause of depression. The Anxiety virus, if not dealt with, will inevitably infect partners, family, friends and children.

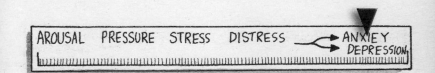

The DEPRESSION virus

(Latin: Joyus Strangulatus)

And, finally, the nastiest of the family - the potentially fatal virus that is the most common end result of stress burnout and anxiety. Everyone gets "down" once in a while, something that is perfectly normal. Being "down" is a normal reaction to dealing with the bad things that life (or some people) throws at us. The illness of depression is much worse than this. Being 'down' doesn't stop us going to work or dealing with family responsibilities; we might feel pretty bad, but we still get on with things even if it's a struggle. When this "down" gets worse however, it interferes **SO** much with our thinking, our emotions and with our behaviour and general health that 'normal' everyday tasks are near impossible to carry out. Sometimes you can just "snap out" of feeling down; not so with the illness of depression.

AROUSAL PRESSURE STRESS DISTRESS → ANXIEY
                                      → DEPRESSION

ANXIETY

Examples of the main anxiety illnesses:

Generalised Anxiety Disorder

Persistent and excessive worry and distress. An exhausting existence leading to everyday problems of coping with work, family and social life. Many physical symptoms. A constant state of over-alertness that is Inappropriate and counter-productive. Disturbed sleeping.

Panic Disorder

Sudden, intense and overwhelming episodes of fear. Panic attacks which are completely immobilising. In between attacks functioning may be OK. Panics include chest pain, dizziness, shortness of breath, churning stomach. Choking sensations and a fear of losing control are common. Fear of death and collapse provoke more panic feelings.

Post Traumatic Stress Disorder

After a stressful event or an exceptionally threatening situation, there may be flashbacks, nightmares, and intrusive (disturbing) memories. Avoidance behaviour, panic feelings and depression can also occur. Increased alcohol and drug taking can become problematic.

Phobic Anxiety

An irrational fear causing major avoidance behaviours. Can produce intense and overwhelming distress, even panic attacks. Life and work activities become restricted, relationships suffer. Common fears include leaving home, open spaces, speaking in public, social events, travelling, animals and insects. Family members, including children become 'roped into' avoidance procedures.

Obsessive Compulsive Disorder

A compulsive ritualistic behaviour that MUST be adhered to - fed by a constant series of recurring thoughts (ruminations) and self-perpetuated 'commands'. Procedures develop (hand washing/tidying/cleaning/organising) that involve increasingly complex and lengthy ritualistic acts, that cannot be stopped or interrupted. Intense feelings of anxiety may follow any interruption of any procedure - which must be started again. Family and children often end up becoming part of the procedures, as participants or witnesses.

There are "CARRIERS" of the stress virus

Perhaps you recognise this in some people you know? We all get "infected" from time to time, but there are some people who are infected ALL the time, carrying the 'virus' wherever they go.

Such individuals spread tension to those around them. The really bad ones don't even know they are doing it. Worse still are the **'TOXIC WASTE SPREADERS'**! These are painful people who spread their pain everywhere. The only thing to do with these folk is to: **STAY AWAY FROM THEM!**

Are there some early signs of infection?

Sure are! Just ask someone what INTERESTS they've got in life. People who are infected with the stress virus have already started giving things up

Everyone has interests (except particularly sad individuals), but they either don't have time for them anymore, are too tired to do them, have lost interest in them (but not replaced them with any new ones), or other things have taken over (e.g. work/kids/TV). The stress virus, if not caught early, causes people to put life 'on hold'. Left unchecked, Jack becomes an empty person, with an empty life; the risk is high of catching the dreaded **'Tedious Maximus'** virus; the **BORING** virus! Without interests, you don't have a life. Your ability to cope is SEVERELY reduced. Having an active (an interesting) life helps you cope and makes life interesting, making YOU interesting. So ask yourself: "What have I stopped doing?"'

The 3 stages of
"Stress BURNOUT!"

It is important at this point to be aware of <u>**2 things**</u> when looking at these 3 stages: - **SEVERITY** (how <u>**bad**</u> is it?), and **DURATION** (How <u>long</u> does it go on for?). Take these 2 things into consideration when looking at these 3 stages, as we **ALL** will recognise certain elements of all 3 stages. There is a big difference between someone who has **Stage 3** symptoms (mild, low severity, short duration, and another who has severe and long-lasting symptoms. Bear this in mind!

On the stress curve, the 3 stages can be seen as such:

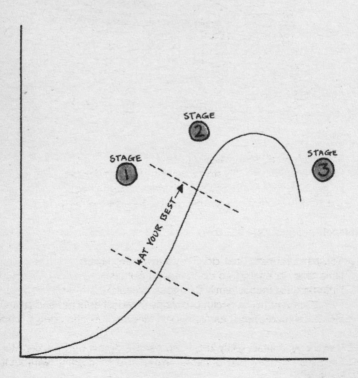

STAGE 1
(The 'Plate Spinning' Stage)

o   Too much work/demands all the time.
o   Functioning high on the stress curve day in and day out.
o   Producing HIGH levels of stress chemicals constantly.
o   The body's chemistry is getting out-of-balance

This commonly produces signs such as:

o   Constant tiredness (that doesn't go away on day off)
o   Little time (or energy) to do interests/hobbies
o   Little time for friends/family (life goes 'on hold')
o   More frequent minor health problems (headaches/aches and pains)
o   Increased medicines (headache/pain relievers), alcohol, drugs, smoking.

The ONE THING that IS intact (only just) is your **sense of humour!** You can still laugh at yourself and see the funny side of things. This is **VITAL** for **coping**. Without it you'll move to **Stage 2!**

STAGE 2

You have now LOST your sense of humour and are functioning VERY HIGH on the stress curve.

Things are **NOT FUNNY** any more! Your ability to cope is severely collapsing - you are producing HUGE levels of stimulant chemicals, resulting in marked physical/mental symptoms:

o   Anger outburst / irritability / moodiness / withdrawal
o   Inability to keep perspective - blowing things out of proportion
o   Experiencing a range of physical and psychological symptoms
o   Sleep / appetite disturbance
o   Intense/serious/preoccupied/recurring worries/no fun
o   Previously calm - now an erupting volcano!

SYMBOLIC BEHAVIOUR

Another common sign of **Stage 2** is **"SYMBOLIC BEHAVIOUR"**. This is behaviour that comes about by repressing unresolved or unpleasant feelings over a long period of time. The 'trigger' might be a trivial thing, but it provokes a HUGE outburst. For example:

This outburst is caused not by the dirty cups. The dirty cups are simply a **trigger** for the built-up emotions that are lurking below the surface. It's easier to get angry at the **cups**, rather than address the **REAL** issues that have been building up (e.g. relationship problems, money worries, health concerns, work pressures etc). See the section about the "SHOPPING TROLLEY"!

STAGE 3

This is not good! You have lost some major ingredients that are needed to cope. **Stage 3** people are <u>very</u> difficult and Pain-Full.

At this stage the person has lost some of the following:

o   INTEREST- has become **'mechanical'**, simply carrying tasks out.

o   PLEASURE - **withdrawal** (physical/emotional). Distant. No fun.

o   ACHIEVEMENT - Feeling **helpless** and **hopeless**. Given up.

Very commonly there is also cynicism about everything (and everyone), rudeness (uncaring and insensitive), rigid attitudes, at best unhelpful…at worst obstructive (and destructive). We can all feel like this from time to time, but if in this mode severely, and for a long period - <u>**it's time to take major stock!**</u>

Are you on the 'HAMSTER WHEEL'?

The more the virus infects you, the <u>MORE</u> you have to:

o   **Keep up, work harder!**
o   **Spin more and more plates!**
o   **Leave your life behind**, become a **SHEEP** (not a hamster)

"Is it time to take stock of things?"

Its all too easy to slip into a way of life that is unrewarding and unfulfilling and that's the problem: it's **EASY**. As time rolls on you find yourself muddling though each day, and 'you' gets <u>lost</u>.

Monday	Tuesday	Wednesday
Got up	Got up	Got up
Got breakfast	Got breakfast	Got breakfast
Went to work	Went to work	Went to work
Got home	Got home	Got home
Made dinner	Made dinner	Made dinner
Had an argument	Had an argument	Had an argument
Watched TV	Watched TV	Watched TV
Went to bed	Went to bed	Went to bed

o   What's happened to your 'life', your 'interests', 'you'?
o   Has it all become uninteresting, dull, unrewarding, but 'safe'?
o   If you like it like this then fine; if you don't, **then maybe you should start to think?**
o   Are you like this to keep others happy, at the expense of your **own** happiness?

But stepping OFF the hamster wheel has risks

For some :

o   It feels too risky
o   It causes a feeling of overwhelming insecurity
o   It means making changes
o   It threatens the status quo (upsets the balance)
o   It means a drop in income, less money, less buying power, less status

Yet, for others:

o   It is liberating
o   It stimulates new ideas, a new future
o   It re-establishes 'old' standards
o   It provides opportunity for change
o   It frees from competing with others

The FUEL GAUGE

If only the human body had some sort of 'fuel gauge', like a car, to monitor how much 'fuel' you had left!

But this is EXACTLY what you need to develop. It has to be DEVELOPED, since we are not born with one. Imagine not having a fuel gauge in your car; you'd inevitably break down! Every so often you look at how much fuel is left. Does it need topping up, or have you got plenty to last? The mind and body are the same; we need monitoring, checking out to see if there's enough fuel to go on, or whether you need a top up. **Self-awareness** and the means to re-charge/top up is something you can learn to develop. If you don't develop this, you too can break down!

What (or who) is your battle with?

Life is a constant battle with relatives, work colleagues, officials, strangers, time, money the kids.

As the viral infections get worse (or remain constant over time), you might become aware of other battles that commence - battles with:

o   Your own emotions
o   Your own thoughts
o   Your own reactions

These sorts of battles can be harder, because they are inside your own head. No wonder some people think they are going "mad", driven to distraction by repeating thoughts that wake them up (or prevent sleep) or by feelings of regret about things said earlier. These battles in your head cause a huge amount of tiredness, frustration, guilt, anguish and **BATTLE FATIGUE!**

Fighting the battle...
in your head

There is no easy answer and we each need to deal with these battles differently, but there are some key BATTLE STRATEGIES worth noting. Even the best Generals don't go into battle without standing back and evaluating the situation and this is the first step.

You MUST stand back & take a look at yourself. Without this you're in trouble! This encourages **'insight'**, your KEY to CHANGE. Without insight **nothing ever changes**, so take your time, look at what you are saying to yourself. Get to know **YOU!**

The dangers of 'BATTLE FATIGUE'

Sometimes the constant battle of getting through the day, battling your own thoughts, fighting with others, can be so exhausting that another state of mind can take over.

When you are tired from battles with others or yourself, it is easier to settle into a more comfortable state of **denial** and **avoidance**. Maintaining this state also maintains the stress however. To change this needs self-examination; developing insight. Are you ready (and willing) to take a look inside yourself?

Getting to know you

Not always comfortable, because you need to look and acknowledge what you're doing right, and what mistakes you may be making. So:

o   Do I recognise there are things I like about me, and need to keep?
o   Do I recognise I do some things that don't help me (or others)?
o   Are there some things I've not really addressed/sorted?
o   If I could, what things would I change?
        What's possible? What's not possible?
o   Can I acknowledge how I feel with someone else? Can I ask for help?
o   Am I able to take a look at myself and monitor how I'm doing?

How about starting a journal or book entitled "ME". This is a book in which you are going to make day to day observations about what you think and how you feel. What feelings fill you up, how you react to these feelings and what you've learned.

LOOK AND LEARN!

The importance of DIET

In our rush to get things done and amidst our tired lives, we stop eating properly. A common cause of tiredness is dehydration - not drinking enough fluids in the day (and this doesn't mean alcohol!). Convenience foods, tinned (and microwaveable) meals and snacks contain far too many preservatives, salt and 'additives'. Fizzy drinks, cigarettes and too much alcohol all contribute to draining the body of the essential ingredients it needs to function and think properly. We'll become more tired, more overweight, less mentally alert and be more likely to suffer major illnesses and die younger. We clog our wonderful bodies up with garbage! Try, for a week, to note down what you eat and drink. Take stock.

The importance of MENTAL DIET too!

It's not just what we physically consume, it's also about what we mentally consume.

Having an occasional 'slob' is OK (quite enjoyable, actually!). But having a daily diet of garbage <u>is not good for the soul!</u> The mind needs stimulation and adventure; a good diet for the mind is essential for coping well, otherwise we become stale and unfit. Children need new experiences and new tastes; as we grow up (and succumb to hectic lifestyles and demands) we fall into habits of under-stimulation, leading to us becoming empty vessels leading empty lives. A perfect breeding ground for the stress virus!

C or G

Convenience

o   Quick (burgers) food, easy (microwave) food.
o   Shop for everything in the one store.
o   Drive everywhere.
o   Computer dating; easy & less effort needed.
o   Order by e-mail; have it delivered.
o   E-mail / text; less face-to-face contact.
o   Sit kids in front of computer game.
o   Watch TV, get a video/DVD.

Or Quality

o   Fresh (local) produce, creative cooking.
o   Use local corner store and individualistic shops.
o   Walk, explore, adventure, new sights and sounds
o   Meet people; say "Good morning".
o   Less e-mail/text; SEE people; spend time with others.
o   Give kids adventurous/creative activities.
o   Go out and develop interests and hobbies

Having more, quicker, has a price. But having less is too high a price for many people who prefer goods, money and materialistic gain. Being rich and having material possessions may NOT bring happiness, but this is now the desire for many. What have you stopped doing? What are you missing out on? What's important to you?

Are you becoming 'HUNGRY' physically and mentally?

Self-medications?

It's inevitable that we 'treat' ourselves first, before seeking further advice or help. What are you taking?

Common self-treatments:

o　　　　Increased alcohol - to relax
o　　　　Increased smoking - to relax
o　　　　Increased medications - painkillers, for the headaches, illegal drugs
　　　　　(e.g.cannabis), to relax
　　　　　Antacids, for indigestion/stomach pains
o　　　　High sugar foods - for the quick fix of energy
o　　　　High energy 'stimulant' drinks - to reduce the tiredness
o　　　　Convenient (high salt/fats) foods - to save time/energy
o　　　　Health foods (vitamins/'natural' additives) - to compensate for the rubbish
　　　　　you eat

Need we say any more? All of these simply make it all worse!
The trouble is, they are easy and convenient. Change needs **effort.**

What <u>ARE</u> the little changes?

Here are some ideas:

Diet?
Amount of tea & coffee?
Fluids?
Amount of alcohol?
Time at work?
Time for me?
Time for friends?
What do I do to relax?
Rest times?
Stops & breaks?
Lunch breaks?
Exercise & activity?
Holiday...time away?
When do I have FUN?
Posture?
Speed I do things?
What have I stopped doing?
Mental diet?
People I have around me?
Sleep patterns?
Try Something New

Don't accumulate your problems

Some people bunch all their problems together, creating a huge, insurmountable massive and immovable, IMPOSSIBLE problem. Instead of having a few problems they now have a **HUGE** PROBLEM.

This is called **THE ELEPHANT!** A huge immovable problem that's simply **"impossible"** to solve. Elephants are difficult , if not impossible to shift.

<u>Never try to tackle an ELEPHANT without breaking it down first!</u>

Making changes

The biggest mistake most people make is to:

o   Make BIG changes straight away.
o   Change TOO MANY things too quickly.
o   Make changes without telling or consulting others.
o   Make the wrong changes.

Also, if you lump ALL the 'problems' you see together, into one big problem, you'll never tackle them! Putting all your discontented 'bits' together, or putting all your problems into one large LUMP, is a bit like trying to tackle an **elephant!** Elephants can't be tackled easily; you should a) get help and b) break the elephant down into manageable parts!

Breaking the elephant down

Don't tackle ALL the problems at once. Slice them down into chunks.

Try the following steps, but take your time with each step:

1.   List ALL your problems small and large.
2.   Now put this list into ORDER: the most difficult, down to the easiest.
3.   From this list take out the INSOLUBLE problems (there are no solutions).
4.   From what's left, choose the smallest or easiest problem to work on.
5.   With this problem, list ALL the possible OPTIONS there are - everything!
6.   Going through each option, now list the advantages & disadvantages.
7.   Having gone through the pro's & con's, now pick which option to tackle
8.   Having now picked an option, work out a detailed PLAN of how to do it.
9.   Now carry it out following your systematic plan.
10.   Once done and worked out, go onto the next problem & do the same.

What about those "insoluble problems"?

Some problems in life simply CAN't be solved - there IS no solution. For example, you CAN'T choose your relatives! There is a famous philosophy worth applying to these insoluble problems, and it's this:

"YOU CAN'T ALWAYS INFLUENCE WHAT OTHERS SAY OR DO TO YOU - BUT YOU <u>CAN</u> INFLUENCE HOW YOU REACT TO IT!"

This recognises that there are many things in life (including people) that you can't influence; life **IS** going to throw things at you that are not fair, people **ARE** going to say things and do things to you that also are not fair, <u>THAT IS LIFE!</u>, but you CAN change HOW YOU REACT TO IT. What this means is that YOU have some things inside you that YOU can change, and these are: your THOUGHTS, your EMOTIONS, your BEHAVIOURS. These are **YOURS**, regardless of outside influences, you **CAN** change these if you want to?

The 'CHINESE WHISPERS' of the mind

In stressful or upsetting events, processes in the body and mind go 'haywire'. The start to distort the normal biological processes (e.g. increasing or decreasing certai chemicals) thereby distorting our thinking and emotional responses. Remember th game 'Chinese Whispers'? That's the one where someone starts a simple phrase a one end of a line of people, but by the time it reaches the last person the initia simple phrase has completely changed into something different.

When we are relaxed and content, and a thought is created, the body, by mean of various natural chemicals (neurotransmitters), transmits this thought through th brain until it reaches conscious thought. The brain creates a thought and produce some chemicals to transmit this thought along a pathway until it reaches you conscious level of thinking.

Calm Process: (Thought) "Did I lock the door?"
Stressed Process: (Amplified thoughts) "Oh No! I didn't lock the door!!"

'Coping' is about reducing the 'CHINESE WHISPERS' effect

Half the battle in tackling stress is about understanding what's going on in the mind and body:

Understanding how the transmission process takes place.
Understanding that certain chemicals can maximise a reaction, or minimise it.
Watching for Chinese Whispers in your <u>own</u> head. <u>Catching them quickly!</u>
Watching how your mood alters the chemical imbalance and the end thought.
Watching you don't misinterpret things/situations/what people say simply
 because you're 'juiced up' or 'watered down'! <u>Your own chemicals can lie to you!</u>

<u>Where</u> does YOUR tension <u>GO?</u>

You will find that when you get a bit too stressed, the tension accumulates in specific places in your body

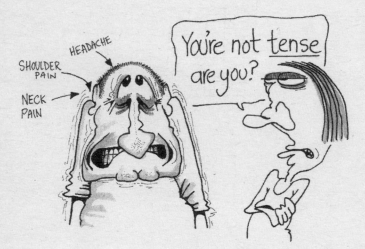

Learn to identify **WHERE** your tension sits and settles.

o   Target this area of your body with movement, exercise, activity, and particularly with regular **massage/heat**.

o   Learn to pick up the <u>early signs</u> that your muscles are beginning to accumulate too much tension. **<u>Massage!</u>**

o   Try to avoid continual use of **painkillers**, you're just masking the problem. If you don't ease it, **it will get worse!**

o   Even **BETTER**, plan into your week/month a regular therapeutic massage. Get it before it gets **YOU!**

Self-monitoring

Start taking a closer look at your day to day mood and tension levels. Are there patterns?

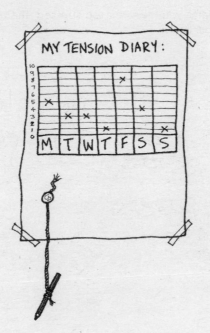

For a few weeks (or longer), take a note of the following:

o   Tension level (on a zero to 10 scale)
o   Mood levels (on a zero to 10 scale)
o   Triggers - what increases/lowers tension and mood
o   After a time are there any regular patterns emerging?

What can you learn from these patterns?
What does your score tell you?

Relaxation

A whole book could be given to this topic (and many good ones are!) because relaxation can be incredibly powerful. There are many relaxation exercises on CD and other media which you can use (see list on page 96)

Relaxation does several important things **VITAL** to controlling tension:

o   It reduces the stimulant effects of adrenaline
o   It reduces blood pressure
o   It increases brain wave activity that is therapeutic
o   It decreases brain wave activity that arouses stress
o   It distracts the mind and creates calmer thought patterns
o   It gives you a few moments out of the rat-race
o   It improves sleep and mood
o   It is pleasant!

Quick "Head-to-Toe" relaxation

Keeping a check on tension involves periodically relaxing the muscles, to allow the physical build up of muscle tension to reduce and improve circulation.

> Relax face, mouth, neck. Relax shoulders. Relax arms, hands, fingers. Relax back, legs... Relax feet and toes...

This exercise only takes a minute or two, well worth the time as it reduces the build-up of muscular tension. It helps improve the circulation (cleansing away the built up salts and increasing blood flow) and balances blood gas levels again. Try to do this several times throughout the day:

1. Close your eyes. Take a slow deep breath...slowly in...slowly out.
2. Relax your face muscles....your eyes... your mouth... your tongue.
3. Relax your neck....slowly rotate your head around in slow circles.
4. Take another slow deep breath.....slow....slow....
5. Tilting your head to the right, slowly roll your head forward until your chin rests on your chest..continue rolling your head (slowly) over to the left, and then backwards - opening your mouth as you tilt your head back. Repeat this in the opposite direction. Take another slow breath.
6. Relax your shoulders (move them around a bit)..relax your neck...
7. Relax your arms...down your arms...relax your hands and each finger.
8. Relax your back...down your legs..to your feet...and right down to your toes.
9. Take another slow breath...slow in...slow out...
10. Slowly run down your whole body, as above, attempting to relax it one last time in each area. Finish with one last deep...slow...breath. Sit still now for a few minutes. When you are ready, slowly get on with what you were doing.

Visualisation techniques

By distracting the mind onto other (more pleasant) things, a more relaxed state will follow. Meditation has been used for centuries to induce a deep state of well-being

Remember those times when you look nostalgically through old photos? For a few minutes you get 'lost' in fond memories. Visualisation is the same, except it is done by using the mind's 'eye'. Sometimes you only need do this for a few minutes. Here are some examples of images to create for yourself:

Take a few quiet moments, and consider creating an image such as:

o   **A holiday you had in the past (with fond and vivid memories)**
o   **An imaginary place (that you would LOVE to visit)**
o   **A real place you've never been to before (but would love to)**

With one of these in mind, think now in MICROSCOPIC detail: what would you see? what are the objects/people, the colours, the sounds - right down to the smallest detail; the sand, the plants, the grasses, the feel of the surfaces, the clouds, the birds, the sound of the breeze. Everything. **Think of everything.** As you do this try and take periodic slow deep breaths; relax, enjoy, the picture.

<u>Use the mental photos you've already got in your own brain's photo album</u>

Biofeedback

This is a tool to help demonstrate how you can actually control tension. It is a device that measures the stress effect via a biofeedback machine. With practice you can learn to control your own biological systems, and it can also help demonstrate how effective your relaxation techniques are.

Zen-Chi

An exercise designed to increase levels of (natural) body chemicals that induce a sense of well-being and relaxation. Lying down, and placing the ankles onto the Zen-Chi machine, the machine (by means of a hand operated timer) moves the body in a wave motion. When the machine stops there is a release of these chemicals through the body producing a pleasant sensation.

Exercise

In depression and low mood, a slow and gradual increase in activity is needed. In stress-related symptoms it is generally better to have bursts of vigorous exercise to burn out the offending chemicals that have accumulated in the body, The resulting increase in endorphins often creates an instant sense of well-being or natural "hIgh". It will also help with sleep (as the body is more naturally tired). Avoid excessive and highly competitive exercise - this might make thIngs worse!

Contact: Your local gym or other like-minded people

Activity

Any activity that brings a sense of **pleasure** and **enjoyment** and **fulfilment**. Creative pastimes are best for this. You don't have to be 'artistic' to be creative. Now is the time to start planning such activities into your life. If an activity you try doesn't take your mind off concerns for a while, then try something that does. Join a class, or learn a language, start badminton, take up pottery, learn about computers, join a hill walking club; anything. Try it.

Contact: Your local leisure centre, library or college.
Look in the newspaper or the internet

Distraction

This is simply a way to distract your mind onto something (anything) else that makes you feel a bit better. Even if you do it for only a few moments

Although it might sound silly, some of the following techniques are used by many professionals with their patients. The point is: if your mind/your thoughts are following a certain path (that's not helpful or even unpleasant), then **DO** something to **SHIFT** your thoughts. A basic principle is that if your mind is working against you, then use ANY other **SENSE** (hearing/taste/touch/sight/smell) to **MOVE your mind AWAY**. This quick shift interrupts the 'bad' thoughts and re-focuses the mind.

The short-sharp-shock methods:
o   Put something into your mouth that is overpowering
         (lemon/lime/citrus/sharp tasting)
o   Smell something overpowering
         (perfume/essential oil/smelling salts/after shave)
o   Keep an elastic band around your wrist....
         pull hard and let it smack your wrist! (but not too hard!)

Other ways to distract:
o   Put on some LOUD music (preferably using a personal sound system!)
o   Run up and down the stairs vigorously
o   Splash water on your face (preferably COLD water)

Start building the qualities of aromatherapy into your day

Alternative therapies

Practised for thousands of years, our ancestors had something right! Try some and find out which ones you like, then plan them into your week.

Consider looking into (and hopefully trying):

o   **Aromatherapy**
o   **Reflexology**
o   **Indian head massage**
o   **Swedish remedial massage**
o   **Reiki**

Apart from simply making you FEEL better, they are likely to lower your blood pressure, reduce muscular tension (and pain), and improve your self-esteem (because you deserve it)! Don't wait for 'permission' from others...plan it.
<u>You can't lose!</u>

Denial. OK for a while, but...

It's not always the right time to address things. Maybe you need to live in a world of denial because:

o You're not ready to deal with the problems
o It's too difficult right now to face the problems
o You don't have the right people around to help you
o You don't know HOW to deal with the problems

So, for a while, maybe you have to just 'sit' on it. However, if you do this for too long:

o You run the risk of becoming ill
o You might be allowing the problem/s to get worse
o You'll start spreading the 'virus' to those around you
o It becomes too 'comfortable' and avoidance becomes normal!

Overcoming denial

This means at the very least acknowledging to yourself that there **IS** indeed a problem. Wouldn't it be great if this were easy?

Consider:

o   Can you **admit** to yourself that there is a problem?
o   Can you **share** this acknowledgement with someone else?
o   Can you **write down** the problem/s and maybe share these too?
o   What might be the a) possible **risks** and b) possible **advantages?**
o   What might be the consequences of **doing nothing?**
o   Are there any personal **advantages/gains** to being too stressed?
o   What is your a) **fear** and b) **hope** of confronting the problem?

Asking for help
Family and friends

Opening up and asking for help is often the most difficult thing to do (particularly for some men). We often try to 'muddle through' it ourselves, which is fine if we can do it. Sometimes it's better to get things out into the open.

It's not necessarily about making HUGE and MONUMENTAL changes (although for some it is), it's more about simply announcing to those around that you are going to try, over the next few months, to make some little changes that will hopefully reduce the pressures and make for a happier day-to-day life (they might even thank you for this!).

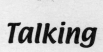

Talking

Start taking a closer look at your day-to-day mood and tension levels. Sometimes, although friends, partner and family might mean well, it is not who you want to talk to. Indeed, sometimes they are the very cause of the tension! Sometimes too, there is a lot to talk about, so perhaps you are building up **TOO** much 'tension'

Is it time to find someone to talk things over with? Perhaps it's not the right time. Maybe that time is somewhere in the future? When the time IS right (and you'll probably know when that is), there are many sources of help available. Consider:

o   **National help/organisations (see page 96).**
o   **Your GP or practice nurse (or health visitor if you're a mum with young children)**
o   **Has your doctor's surgery got access to a counselling service?**
o   **Your GP can refer you to an accredited counsellor or psychologist.**
o   **Look yourself: try the British Association of Counselling (see page 96).**
o   **Chat with friends and see if they know of someone (check they are accredited).**
o   **Your local religious leader?**

Many people get a great sense of well-being from spiritual guidance, prayer and sharing concerns or problems. Sharing with anyone in whom you trust is good. Someone from outside sees things differently.

Medical help?

Many years ago there was a great 'craze' on medical treatments for stress and anxiety, namely things like tranquillisers. There were (and still are) problems with these.

Tranquillisers were over-prescribed and the result was decades of dependant users, still with the same problems! Tranquillisers are NOT the answer. They are still used, but the lessons have (mainly) been learned. They are highly addictive and tend to simply mask the real problems. They can be helpful in **small** doses for **short** periods of time, for a **small** number of people. It is generally accepted now that medication is not the first port of call; a skilled GP giving the proper advice, reassurance and information is as effective as any tranquilliser for people with mild to moderate problems.

Seeing your GP

Before seeing your doctor, it can be really helpful to work some things out beforehand. Don't go in with dreaded "VAGUE SYMPTOMS"

It is helpful to both yourself and the doctor, to outline exactly what the problem is. Consider writing a (short) list of your (main) symptoms. Include some idea of how long it's been going on, how bad it is, how it interferes with your day to day life, and even (if you have some idea) of the causes or 'triggers'. It can also be helpful to ask the receptionist (or practice manager) which is the best doctor to see; all have their own specialities and interests.

<u>Don't be disappointed if your GP doesn't give you tablets!</u>

Sometimes <u>certain</u> medications can be helpful

GP's rarely prescribe tranquillisers, but there are now safer and non-addictive medications available. Your doctor might prescribe a low-dose antidepressant, as these also have (apart from their mood lifting effects) a relaxing effect (called a sedative). This can be helpful for people who have sleep problems. Your doctor will explain this. These medications do have some side effects but are not addictive.

Always tell your doctor if you are taking any other preparation (e.g. from a health food shop) as some of these can interact with prescribed tablets. It is better however, to tackle this without tablets.

'Natural' remedies?

Many people try a range of things before seeking further help, and there are many items available for 'stress', however some are better than others.

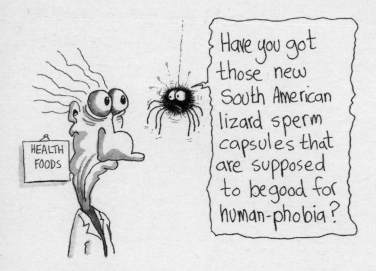

There is some evidence that St John's Wort (Hypericum) helps with mild to moderate depression and for some stress related symptoms. For improving sleep and creating calmness, Passiflora and extract of wild Lettuce are popular. Some of the highly marketed brands can be mainly filled with sugar and/or non-therapeutic substances. Try and seek advice from a professional regarding these. They are, however, worth trying before resorting to too much alcohol! Don't make 'cocktails' of many substances!

Life adjustments

'erhaps it's more about taking stock of things and making some small 'adjustments':

- **Taking** more time for yourself on a regular basis
- **Making** time for partner, family, the children, friends etc
- **Forcing** yourself to STOP more; have breaks, lunch, time to relax.
- **Building** into your day more, pleasurable activities.
- **Trying** new things, making small changes in routine
- **Creating** opportunities, e.g. meeting new people, new interests
- **Changing** diet, routine, thoughts, reactions, posture

Sometimes it is indeed about making major lifestyle changes.

<u>WHO</u> *do you have around you?*

Surrounding yourself with people who do you **NO** good, is a perfect environment for the stress virus to multiply! Why not surround yourself with:

o **Miserable people**
o **People who always 'take' (not givers)**
o **Complainers**
o **Demanding people**
o **Snobs or condescending people**

- and see what happens! Watch how you get <u>**DRAINED**</u> very quickly!

"DRAINS"

These are people who, quite literally, **drain** you

So, consider:

o   Taking a look at the <u>types of people</u> who are in your '<u>space</u>'?
o   How do these people make you <u>feel</u>, what do they give you?
o   Can you <u>create more distance</u> from these people?
o   If necessary can you get these people <u>out of your life</u> completely?

Sometimes it's as if some people are waiting for 'permission' to eliminate some of these 'drains' from their lives. **You don't need such permission!** Have more '<u>radiating</u>' people around you!

"RADIATORS"

These are the sorts of people you need around you more! Some Drains are unavoidable, but you **can** make more of a **conscious effort** to reduce time with the drains and have more radiators in your life:

o   **Vibrant and energetic people**
o   **Creative and inspirational individuals**
o   **Optimistic and practical people**
o   **Giving and caring people**
o   **People who make you feel good**

"How's <u>YOUR</u> fuse?"

We're all different, with different characters and different personalities and have learned different ways of coping and reacting. Some people just have a **SHORT FUSE**.

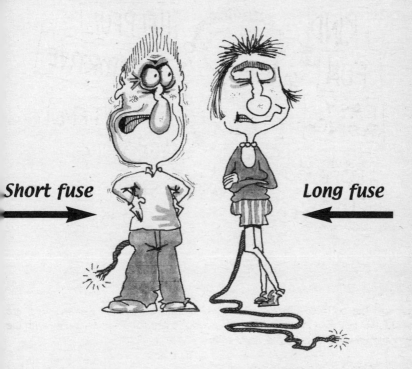

Short fuse →   ← **Long fuse**

Stress shortens your fuse (however wonderful you are)! So keeping a check on your stress levels will have an effect on how quickly you 'blow'. You CAN develop a longer fuse (if you want to), but it takes:

o   Self-awareness, understanding and watching yourself.
o   Learning from previous 'triggers' and previous reactions.

Practising saying "STOP"/learning quick relaxation/count to 10

Bring yourself <u>down</u> on the stress scale, just a notch or so

Sometimes a particular moment can be overwhelming or difficult. Try to force yourself 'down' a notch on the stress scale.

Try this: On a scale of 0 to 10 (where 0=the most relaxed you've EVER been, and 10=the most tense you've EVER been in you life).

0 _____ 10

  (The most RELAXED   (The most TENSE
   you have ever been)   you have ever been)

1)   Where are you RIGHT NOW on this scale?
2)   <u>**WHY**</u> are you <u>here</u> and not at a higher number on the scale? (i.e. what are you doing <u>**right**</u>, that has stopped you being higher on the scale?)
3)   What could you do **<u>NOW</u>** to bring yourself down by one notch (even if it were only for a few moments)? DO IT, NOW! See if <u>YOU</u> can bring yourself down, even for a few moments.

<u>You CAN influence your tension level!</u>

Saying "NO" is not always easy either for you or others

ome people say "YES" to every request that's thrown at them. They know they nould say "NO" more, but it's too difficult , or causes others to react in a way that simply not worth it! Try some of the following:

Let me think about that and I'll get back to you" (Delays things a bit nd can help you to come up with a reason/answer that is better for you)

Sorry, but I can't help you this time, maybe next time" (Perfectly reasonable)

I'd really like to help, but I just can't at the moment" (Perfectly reasonable)

Sorry, but no I can't" (Perfectly reasonable)

on't feel you have to give <u>reasons</u> and <u>explanations</u>; try to be pleasant, but Ion't automatically say "Yes". Also, don't be overly <u>apologetic</u>! **Practise!**

Making others aware of your state...

It's always difficult, particularly in a busy workplace, to try and make others aware of how busy or 'stressed' you are, to try and keep others at arm's length for a while. Try making a sign like a traffic signal and either put it on your door, or have it on your desk.

Put a moveable paper-clip beside the 'signal':

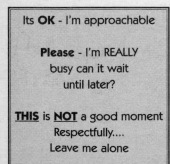

Its **OK** - I'm approachable

Please - I'm REALLY busy can it wait until later?

THIS is **NOT** a good moment Respectfully.... Leave me alone

Perhaps everyone could have one of these - a **team** tool?

Just make sure you **change** it periodically; don't leave it on 'Leave me alone' **all** the time!

A last word from the author

So, stress is normal - we need it.
Too much stress sustained over time
can lead to physical and mental problems.
Stress, in the right appropriate place is
helpful - but in the wrong place is
unhelpful and can damage our lives.
You can influence stress levels by
managing yourself and your life better.
Sometimes its about managing your own
emotions better. There are some
things we can change....and some we
can't. Taking a good look at ourselves
develops insight - the primary thing
you need to make changes. And if
all else fails, practise saying "SOD IT".

RESOURCES

BOOKS
"SOD IT! The Depression 'Virus' and how to deal with it" by Martin Davies
Pub Sod It! Books, PO Box 1, Wirral CH47 7DD, UK.
www.sod-itbooks.co.uk ISBN: 9781901910230

"What Stress: Manual for Workplace stress" by Ruth Chambers & Martin Davies
ISBN 0850842492

"Manage your Mind" by Gillian Butler & Tony Hope
ISBN 978-0198527725

"Who Moved my Cheese?" by Dr Spencer Johnson
ISBN 9780091816971

CDs & TAPES:
o   The Relaxation Kit (CD or Cassettes)
o   Coping with Stress at Work (CD or Cassettes)
o   Coping with Anxiety (CD or Cassette)
o   Coping with Depression (CD or Cassettes)
o   Feeling Good (CD or Cassettes)

All CDs and Tapes from: Talking Life, PO Box 1, Wirral CH47 7DD, UK
www.talkinglife.co.uk Tel: 01516320662

ORGANISATIONS:
THE STRESS MANAGEMENT SOCIETY: Non profit body organised by Professionals & Therapists;
offers information and advice www.stress.org.uk Tel: 08701-999235

COMBAT STRESS: Support organisation for ex services personnel
www.combatstress.org.uk Tel: 01372-841600

NATIONAL PHOBICS SOCIETY: Help and advice on phobias, including links to local self help
groups. www.phobics-society.org.uk Tel: 0870-1222325

DEPRESSION ALLIANCE is the leading UK charity for people affected by depression.
0845 123 23 20 www.depressionalliance.org 212 Spitfire Studios, 63 - 71 Collier Street,
London N1 9BE Email: information@depressionalliance.org

SAMARITANS: Telephone: 08457 909090 Text: 07725 909090
email: jo@samaritans.org www.samaritans.org

Royal College of Psychiatrists, Useful online mental health resource. www.rcpsych.ac.uk

British Association for Counselling & Psychotherapy.
For names & contact details of qualified counsellors: www.bacp.co.uk

Aleph 1, (Biofeedback machines) Bottisham, Cambridge, UK
Tel: 01223811679

Zen-Chi:
www.zenlifestyles.com

YOURSELF: You are your **OWN** resource...never forget what is already inside waiting to
be accessed and used!